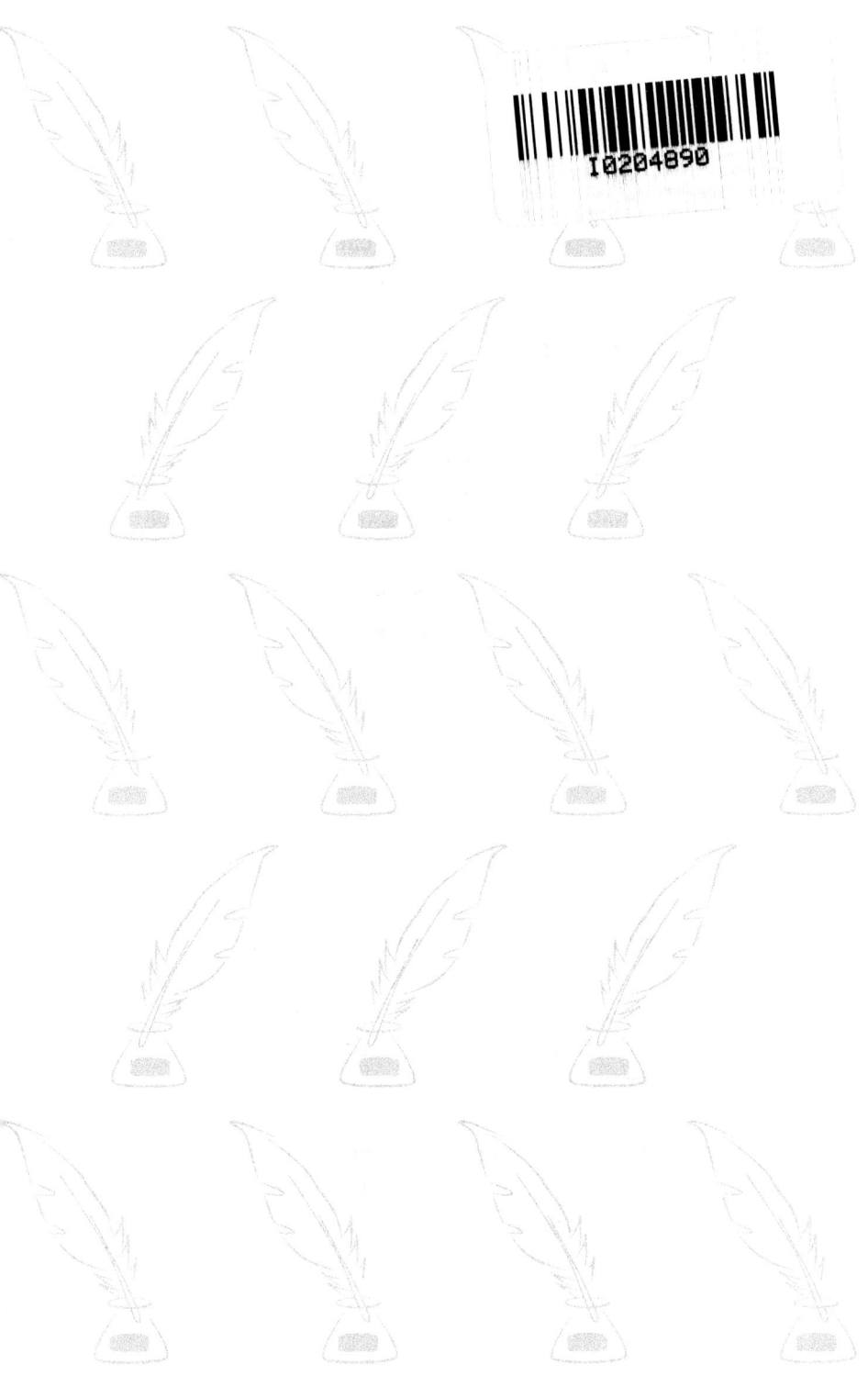

This book is dedicated to:
My friend **Catherine McLaren Stannard**
for introducing me to the power of words;
Janis Cheney 1951-2019 for teaching me,
and the Painted Ladies writers group,
to embrace the journey;
my children **Emily, Benjamin & Matthew**
for all of the love, tears and laughter
they have graced me with in this life;
and as always, for **David**, my love
who walks through this world by my side,
holding hands through tears and laughter.

Copyright © 2019 Dawn Noelle Archer
All rights reserved.
No portion of this book may be reproduced,
distributed, or transmitted in any form
or by any means without prior, express
written permission of the publisher.
For permission contact: Shared Story Press ®
www.sharedstorypress.com
ISBN: 978-1-7323274-2-9

Remnants of Soul

By: Dawn Noelle Archer

Shared Story Press®

Table of Contents

Poems of Youth 1
- Treasures 2
- Why 4
- Remember 5
- Paradise 6
- Scooped 9
- Running 13
- Catch-Up 16
- Summer Solstice 18

Poems of She 21
- Remnants 22
- Marge Piercy 24
- Nothing But 26
- I See You Also 28
- Time Lapse 30
- Her Time 34
- This Is It 36

Poems of He 39
- Connected 40
- He Knows 42
- Down On His Luck 44
- Perhaps 46

Poems of Love 49
- Needs 50
- One 52
- Yellowtail Dam 53
- For David 54
- Simple Gift 56
- Becoming 57

Poems of Change 59
    Burned 61
    Ever Changing 62
    Words 64
    Transformed 65

Poems of Nature 67
    The Land Remembers 68
    Flames of Fall 70
    The City 72
    The River 74
    The Naked Trees 76
    Something 78
    The Prairie 80

Poems of Peace 83
    Peace Is 84
    World Peace 87
    Kindred Spirits 90

Poems of Loss 93
    Come to You Anew 95
    That Space 96
    The Shape of Sadness 98
    Closer Look 100
    I Will Remember 102

Poems of Justice 105
    Cultivate 106
    Kind 109
    The Dance 113

Poems of Youth

Treasures

every morning
the man
fills his pockets with
important things
useful things
things to remind him
what he has become
a handful of coins
pocket knife
wallet
business cards
breath mint
every morning
the boy
fills his pockets with
important things
useful to few perhaps
a penny or two
pieces of a broken toy

crumpled paper
lint-covered candy
pockets are important
when you're 4 or 40
you must have pockets and
they must be filled with
treasures
though I wonder
does the boy
emulate the man
he will one day
become
or the man hold on
to the boy
he was once

Why

a twinkle
in their eyes
enthusiasm
in their voices
they unleash the
knowledge
of the
world
with a single
question

Remember

go to a park
today and
listen to a child
giggle
remember
the sound well
tomorrow that giggle
will only be
the hint of child
in the laughter of
an adult

Paradise

paradise
not one place
not location specific
rather
individually defined
sand sea or sun
perhaps but
waves of feeling always
for me
snuggled up close
face-to-face
big warm bed
grandma's handmade quilt
small hands caress tiny circles
on my cheek
pacifier whispers between
soft giggles & toothy grins
until big blue eyes drift off to sleep
an afternoon nap
with my girl of one

*or the back yard
within a child's pup tent
resting beneath rays of
colorful muted sun
gentle breeze & buzzing bees
soft words of favorite stories
the heart has memorized
an afternoon nap
with my boy of two*

Scooped

play
can be
work
can be
play
perhaps
age matters in
determining
these things
but shouldn't
many full
moons ago
he looked
just innocent
enough
this child

working or
playing
with his vibrant
imagination
grand
vocabulary
and pail
full of sand
shovel
at the ready
innocence radiated
from him like
sunshine
except one
moment
sand filled shovel
hovered
just above
her unsuspecting
head

in a quick stride
or two I
scooped him up
carried him away
wuare am I go-in
he said
four simple words
now
woven forever
in the tapestry
of my life
often wonder that
myself
days and years
grains of sand
slip quickly by
where am I
going

Running

just three and
running away again
upstairs packing
parental transgressions
real or imagined
drive her to run once
or twice per month
it's genetic I'm
told her daddy
ran too at her age
peeking in the room
she has her tiny
red suitcase
going to grandma's
it says
like her daddy did
she's not
both grandmas live
in other states

she's forgotten
some things but
has 3-year-old essentials
small pillow
tuffy her stuffed puppy
favorite books markers paper
a few slices of cheese
hhhmmm
not a long trip then
I ask if she'd like
to take clothes
I get the eye but
she grabs a sweater
out the door she goes
I phone the neighbor
her usual destination but
at the sidewalk she turns
up hill not down
from the window
I watch her sit near
the lilac row

clutching tuffy
she eats some cheese
closes the suitcase
strides for home
I phone the neighbor
ten minutes give or take
on good terms for now
I help her unpack
we nap together
she snuggles up to me in sleep
later she will matter-of-factly
tell daddy
I ran away today
he will nod solemnly
eyes full of mirth as he
remembers his own running

Catch-Up

room full
8-year-olds
riding the last waves
today's stimulant
youth in general
merged with friday
summer break pending
with just a splash of
school wide
pandemonium
um
special program
in the gym
but deadlines loom
she tries
to re-focus energies
complete the task at hand
we need to work hard
she says

we've fallen behind a bit
have to play catch-up
from the back of the room
rising just above the din
wiggling bodies
rustling papers
a lone voice
pure in tone
quietly sings
ketchup, ketchup, ketchup
smiling she looks up
scans the room
seems she's the only one
aware of his punchline
she spots him
dark haired dark eyed
boy of song
impish grin upon his face
he completes the assignment

Summer Solstice

    bedtime
        no
    you have to
        why
    because I said so
        that's notta real reason
    wait did you roll your eyes
    listen it's eight
    you go to bed at eight
        I can't
    why not
        cuz it's not black-dark yet

what
>	outside
>	it's not black-dark
>	I go to bed when it's black-dark
>	see it's still only blue-dark
>	momma you know that

fine
but then in winter
you have to go to bed at five
>	no

why not
>	cuz I go to bed at eight

this child

Poems of She

Remnants

*bits of
memories
of myself or
someone
else
I remember
well
on occasion
perhaps not
who I am
now
but
who I was
once*

*when youth taken
long for granted
was part of
my body
not just
remnants
of my mind
weird business this
life cycle*

Marge Piercy

she who is
daughter woman poet
not necessarily in that order
embraces nothing as if it were
everything and everything as if
life depended upon it
she loves the habitual
questions the incredible
tries to glue them
together with words
she records the world around her
with every particle of her being
reflects it back to us in ways
we begin to understand

she speaks of anything
we say oh yes
I meant that too
she gives to us what we
have been searching for
wrapped in words we
would have used if
poetry had been our
native tongue

Nothing But

was nothing but a dream
in that place in between
what passes for
life and death
nearly awake though
not near enough
to remember
the words
that were whispers
or shouts
so hard to tell
now
but last night
I danced
with the spirit of the plains

and we laughed
when
I couldn't
remember her name
near enough awake
to know
she is real
and I am nothing
but
I dream

I See You Also

I was born
in the wrong place
in the wrong time
among the wrong people
how else to explain
my inability to fit
as a piece
in the puzzle
I find myself
my place is everywhere
but here
my time is eternal
my people are of open
minds and hearts
my children are dance
poetry & music
don't you know by now
each bird has a different song
I must sing and fly
not just search out food

nurturing is akin to nourishment
if I take part in ritual
let the ritual change
or if the ritual be the same
let me be changed
on occasion we cross paths
old souls in new bodies
heartbeats of recognition
upon each encounter we say
I see you
I see
you
then we are gone
once more
me living
in the wrong place
how else to explain

Time Lapse

when
my mother was
young
her house
didn't have indoor
plumbing
outhouse and sears
catalog
enough said about
that
in later years stood
a lone tv
black & white
the phone
a party line
no one to call
anyway
when
I was young

one bathroom
small
shared
sears
brick & mortar
tools and appliances
mostly
two tvs
color
cable optional
rabbit ears no remote
roof top antenna
phone corded
long tangled stretched
thin
into the next room
long distance rates apply
nights and weekends or
do not try
will you accept the charges

when
my daughter was
young
two bathrooms no waiting
sears going going going
casualty of an online world
tvs in most rooms
bigger screens
color cable multiple remotes
phones cord-less
internet connection
old school
dial-up
sorry disconnect
I need to make a call
doo, doot, doot, doo, doot, doot, doo
beep, beep, beep,
kchsh-ooooooooo-sh-sh-sh
houston we have a problem
oops wrong
generation

now
bathrooms are spas
sears
gone nearly
tvs can be anything
go anywhere
phones = cellular
phones = computers
phones = cameras
what is long distance
after all
in a world of unlimited plans
social media connects
and disconnects
more words used
though
of less value
houston we have a problem
kchsh-ooooooooo-sh-sh-sh

Her Time

each night
dusk
is her reward
following
years of daylight
obligations
and darkness
the magic boon of
in-between hours
finds her pressing
each moment
extracting life's essence
she sings a new song
without betraying
old lyrics

*her soul experiences
winter melt
spring is a hymn
well remembered
burst of clarity
pure revelation
blue-black of night
a childish enemy
moments between
darkness and light
become a flood
of self
awareness*

This Is It

she passes
by the old
red door
daily
as she
wanders and
wonders
the door stands
in the middle of
nowhere of importance
and the center of
everything of value
to those who notice
take heed
this is it she thinks
as far as I've ever been
ever

she knows
this side of the door
however arbitrary that seems
on this side of the door
habit resides yet
life awaits
just beyond
the farthest place
one has ever been
she need only
open the door
take one step

Poems of He

Connected

he was
himself
art
body in motion
like watching
music
or hearing
life
his essence
beats within my soul
I was connected
to him
so long ago

I can't remember
when or how or
why only
he's necessary
to me
the words I say
were feelings
long before
I was born

He Knows

he is in the driveway
shooting baskets
with his grandson
he knows
boys at the cusp of
manhood
wish not
to hear the tales
of old men so
they play the game
each basket a link
to the past
he does not see
the wrinkled hands only
net and ball and boy

he does not
smell the ligament
only the excitement
of sport
it beads on his face
tomorrow he will pay
for this folly as
his old body scolds
him for youthful
indiscretions
but for a few
moments
he is
who he was
once

Down On His Luck

everything he owns
rests for now
just at his feet
appearing
wholly insubstantial
in the vast wilds
of western australia
he pokes at
a small fire
as it struggles
the way life has
poked at him
to the point of
bursting into blaze
or dying out
an ember

the thin smoke line
cries out his signal
notice me damn it
notice me
I'm still here
he finds himself
down on his luck
in a place
only the trees
give a care

Perhaps

looking at an old photo
of a little boy
who grew to a man
now gone
I wonder
who did he wish to be
what were his dreams
I never asked the man
fear held me back
perhaps he would think
the questions foolish
or me
for the asking
perhaps he was so busy
day-to-day
breathing and living
he believed no one interested
in the boy he was once

perhaps that is why
the quiet questions
of my eyes
were never answered
with his words
I regret that
it's too late now
to ever know the boy
or the man
I am left
with only photos
of a little boy
who had promise
and a quiet man
who had memories and
so many thoughts
that begin with
perhaps

Poems of Love

Needs

tonight
stay with me
but leave me alone
lay by my side
but don't touch me
touch me
but don't understand me
understand me
but don't know me
know me
but don't speak to me
speak to me
but remain silent
remain silent
and let me speak

let me speak
but don't listen
listen
but don't nod in compliance
nod in compliance
and stay with me
tonight
because I need you here
but want to be alone

One

we danced
a daring dance
until two
became one
neither separate
nor whole
quite resembling
one body with
several minds

Yellowtail Dam

one glance
begins a lifetime
of joint expectation
blue eyes dance
across the water
as ripples of flirtation
echo fish stories told here
pass the libation
drop a line not to worry
love's the journey
not the destination

For David

december 28
1991
the minister said
two shall become one
this morning
I watched you sleeping
knowing
what he meant
just as I have a
right hand and
left hand I have
you
just as I have
a need to breathe
I have a need
for you
just as I have life
I have you

*without you
I am not quite
me
I never
want to be
less than
the sum of
you and I*

Simple Gift

don't apologize
for yesterday
I remember
only the good
don't promise me
tomorrow
it's not yet yours
to give
rather
share with me
your pleasure in
living this journey
today
peace I have
in knowing
hours with you
whiled away

Becoming

two
individual
seeds
planted
side-by-side
in the same
garden
entwining
together
taking on new
shape
becoming more
beautiful
with each passing
year

Poems of Change

Burned

flickering light
chased away
shadows like a
hesitant hero
daring their return
flame danced free
as a child
within confines
always searching
for a way out
wax melted
gave
as a woman
never knowing when
to stop or what
would be left
in the end

Ever Changing

caught I am
in the web of
personal experience
the here
and now
what I see
I believe
has always been
always will be yet
life is ever
changing
to everything
there is a history
each place
each being
each object
a time before
existence
an origin story
added layers

progression
this place
small city today
yet half century ago
wheat fields
150 years
untouched prairie
couple hundred million
years sea covered
four billion years
nothing but
possibility
today
overlooking
acres of asphalt
shimmers of heat
I imagine waves
I see wheat
or water
and I believe

Words

I spill my words
on paper
surround myself with them
wrap words around me
like a cloak
to protect myself
I huddle in their mass
until
the old words no longer fit
perhaps I've outgrown them
or the color is wrong
or I no longer
recognize myself
wearing them
perhaps
I'll weave a new cloak
more encompassing than the last
using fibrous words
of new experience
entwining threads
of old

Transformed

humans climbing
from hammock cocoons
post nap
not unlike caterpillars
turned butterflies
breaking free
of protective covers
butterflies look prettier
exits more graceful
but
both are refreshed
transformed
for the day ahead

Poems of Nature

The Land Remembers

back in the 50's
a man broke a stretch
of montana ground
where an adequately sized house
of function if not form
joined the landscape
the antelope watched and wondered
the sheep grazed not caring at all
the land absorbed the intrusion
and healed the best that it could

grass grew
the family too
flowers trees vegetables
and crops were planted
the land rejoiced and was fruitful
except when it wasn't
over the years heartbreak and
celebration would trade places
more frequently than can be imagined
if one was born another died

when flowers bloomed
drought or grasshoppers
soon followed
generations and decades later
that family gave up on the land
or perhaps
embraced it differently
they moved to town
sold the clueless sheep
tore the old house down
and said goodbye to the wondering antelope
a dirt road to nowhere
points the way
to a history with few relics
save a length of barbed wire fence
guarding nothing
but
the land remembers

Flames of Fall

flames of fall
lick the sky
gasping
last
effort
to impress
the eye
feed the soul
feed the earth
biding til
spring
await rebirth
life bursting
new
green
sun dappled
grace

but eyes
remember
and
minds dance
with
fiery flames
before
fall leaves
are
tamed

The City

the walking me
on a bike path
sidling by
a light rail track
living fence of trees
to the left
nearly
obscures my view
or not of
the concrete jungle
beyond
of business and residence
oceans of asphalt
cars and people
every make and model
here
in this city
birdsong competes
with varied sounds of
transport

*falling light
of sun and moon
diverted
competes with buildings
that stretch to touch
the sky
from where it comes
nature competes
with civilization
intricately designed
strategically placed
flowers only
where we deem them
grow
a scattered seed rarely
finds purchase*

The River

river
watches
patience of a mother
on her side
as we build dams
here and there
convincing ourselves
we control
everything
deep
mountain snowpack
record setting rains
mean nothing
to dam builders
houses with a view
we like
water's edge is
big business
she chuckles
rises

forces releases
spillway gates open
hundreds of thousands
of gallons per second
millions of sandbags
miles of levies
downstream worries
unexpected
they say
really
but
river rises
reminds us
water was here first
water will remain
even
when the last
vestiges of our
control
wash away

The Naked Trees

they stand
these sentinels
out of time
alone
in the middle
of open fields
a view of everything yet
nothing to watch over
or
in the middle
of a forest yet
steeped in aloneness
stripped as they are
of their grandeur
leaves
seed pods
fruit
they've borne
even bark

standing
just standing
naked
grey
smooth
scarred
by insects
birds
time itself
little to offer
but a
temporary perch
cast shadow
glimpse of sky
telling stories
few remember for
the naked trees
have died

Something

there is
something just
something
an honor
really
bearing witness
to the circle
life
living things
in full growth
and glory
potential
bursts
blossoms
with wild abandon
nature's zeal
yielding only to
abundant harvest
blaze colored
crowns and canopies

give way to ember
graceful fall
descent to death
or not death
hibernation merely
resting
this state of
waiting
in cool
quiet
darkness
for something
life sparks
new
green
tender
there
just there
is something

The Prairie

and so it is
you sit on the open prairie
listening to the wind
whisper names of those
whom you do not know
whom you have never known
oddly this comforts you
this knowing you are here
because of them
and so it will be
a hundred years from now
someone new
will sit on the prairie and
listen to the wind
they will hear your name
among the whispers
and be comforted

so it has always been
unknown souls
of yesterday
offering comfort
to those who know
how to listen

Poems of Peace

Peace Is

peace
is a river
mid-summer
in lazy gentle
flow again
after the torrent of
spring thaw
stirs and clouds
our view of
what is
and
what can be

peace is
the moment
cloudy clarifies
the moment that
what we have been
looking at is
reflected
back at us and
we truly
see

World Peace

*world peace
now there's an unrealistic idea
we can't even agree on religion
or healthcare
fossil fuels or renewable energy
paper or plastic
world peace
don't make me laugh
but
what if
we set our standards lower
what if
we started smaller*

what if
my goal was
me peace
and your goal was
you peace
and together we started
we peace
and we could invite her and him
she peace and he peace
together
they peace
and we could all have
us peace
and our us peace could spread
like a cold or a secret

and soon we could have
church peace
and school peace
and work peace
and neighborhood peace
and we could aim higher
and think bigger
and have city or town peace
and state peace
and nation peace
so what if
we can't have world peace
maybe we can have
majority peace

Kindred Spirits

tolerance
is a $5 word
gracelessly
thrown around
impersonating peace
tolerating is
merely putting up with
tolerance is hate invited
through the back door
sitting down to have
coffee no
tolerance
is not peace
peace is
a kindred spirit of
acceptance respect love

peace is
agreeably disagreeing
peace is me
being me
you
being you
them being
them
peace is
each of us holding on
to our beliefs
without letting go
of our
humanity

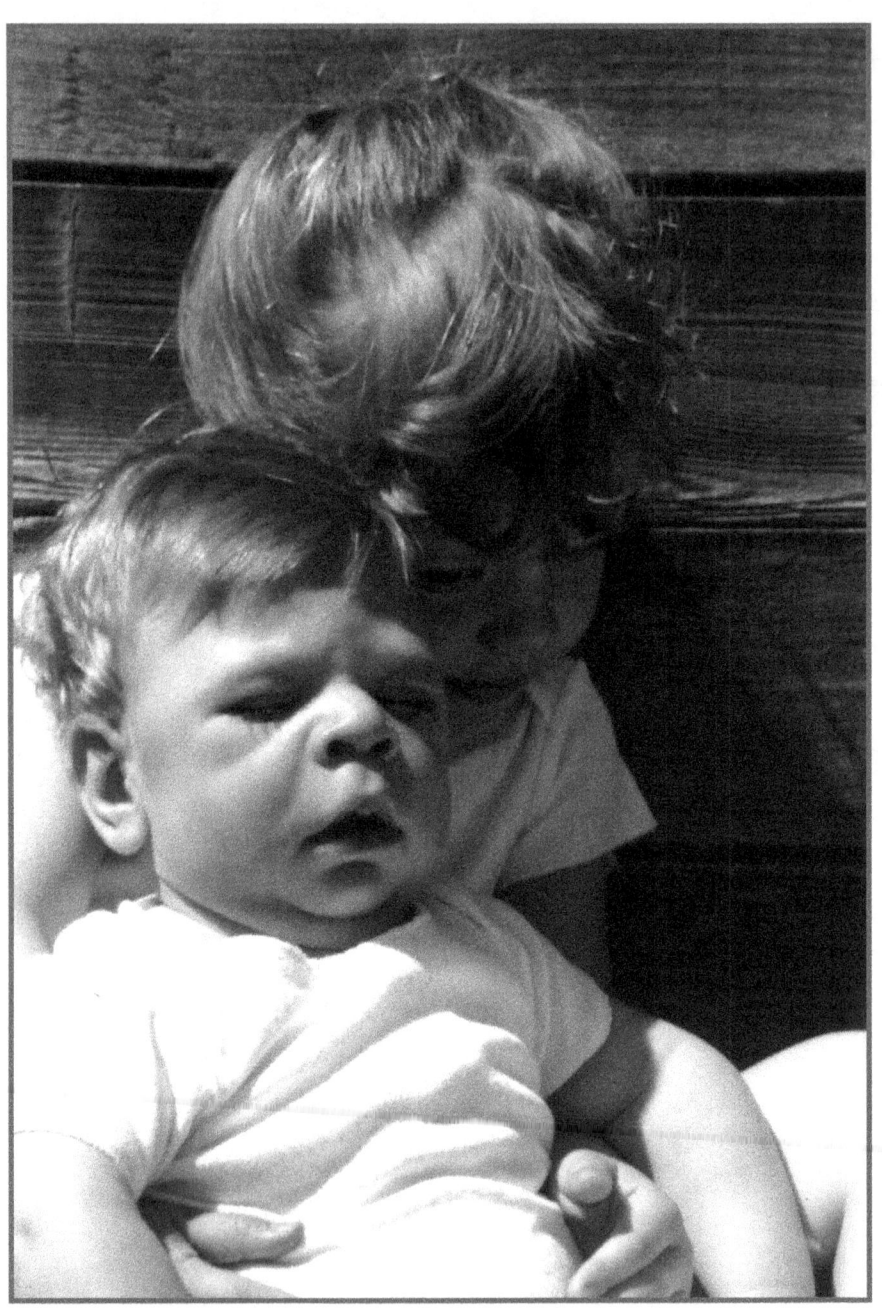

Poems of Loss

Come To You Anew

this day
return me to the earth
my ending
and so my beginning
scatter me where you will
planting me deep
in your collective souls
shed your tears
that your grief may
nurture my memory
though I be silent now
watch for me
in the springs of this life
I will come to you
anew

That Space

cleaning a closet
rarely touched
over the years
attempts made
venture in
sort piles
leave again
but
my child
he lives
in that space
in small pieces
independent
of his body
now gone

deciding
what to keep
what to let go
is hard
harder still
deciding
where to store
what remains
so I never
run across
unprepared

The Shape of Sadness

she wears
loss and grief
daily
sometimes a scarf
offering warm hug
which on occasion
strangle holds
without warning
other times
a purse
colored as her mood
can be set down
briefly
nearly forgotten
yet
something
feels missing

the weight of presence
even temporarily
removed from shoulders
often
favorite jeans
whose lines
have softened
over time accepted
the shape of her
colors of
muted bruise
pockets stuffed with
tearful reminders of
long ago days

Closer Look

maybe
we could stop pretending
that everyone is all right
that no one hurts
that depression
isn't real
that mental health issues
don't exist
that a smile on the outside
means everything
that someone may
be dying to die
maybe
we knew him or her
maybe
we didn't

he kept his pain
hidden behind comedy
she kept her sadness
masked by laughter
their whirlwind of activity
blurred our vision
to pain's reality
maybe

I Will Remember

I will remember
you
though place may change
and routines scatter
written words
will bridge the gap
I will remember
you
distance cannot change that
whilst years surrender
and journeys differ
as others come and go
I will remember
you
time be no obstacle
should age or illness
rob me
of memories bygone
names and faces elude me
a blank stare my reply

no matter
my heart will remember
you
our friendship
a beloved song of old
I will remember
I will
remember
I will remember
you

Poems of Justice

Cultivate

the worst thing
that has ever happened to you
is just that
the worst thing that has ever
happened
to you
you can't use your worst thing
as the measure
for another's worst thing
you can't tell someone
their worst thing
isn't so bad
because
your worst thing was
so much worse
and you can't say
their worst thing isn't real
simply because
it hasn't been your experience
or your reality

but you can
and should
use your worst thing
to cultivate empathy
within yourself

Kind

social media posts
full of adults
ranting
we just need
to teach the children
to be kinder
to not bully
this
from the generations
who openly called men
nancy and women
butch
gay people
fags and dykes
unmarried mothers
sluts
mentally challenged people
retards
those with mental health challenges
bat shit crazy

and everyone
not like them
wierdos
and so many many
many words
for
those of color
different religions
different ethnicities
even today
just be kind adults
find themselves at
youth sporting events
shouting profanities at
children
coaches
referees
about a game
about
a
game

don't forget road rage
because we can't
even be kind
while we drive
the world
full of adults
failing to adult
calling each other
horrific things
our children have heard
words recorded
for the history books
so there's that
where
from whom
did we want children
to learn
just be
kind

The Dance

I stand in the middle
town of
affluent recreation
flathead lake and
mission mountains
behind me looking
across the road
cherry stand
mounds of fruit
fresh from trees
gleam in sunlight
beckoning
the likes of me
above the scene
hovers
the dancing balloon man
bright red inflatable
full of nothing
but air

eternal victim of his
manufactured smile
shoulder of the road
a man lies prone
head propped
on dusty bedroll
homeless hitchhiking
or both
sleeping or passed out
no handmade cardboard requests
pleas of help or destination
sign of the times approaches
jogging stroller sporting
infant and toddler
mother on phone
deep in conversation
notices not
her children
nor their surroundings

the toddler gazes
down upon
human form
in the dirt
thinking
what
as the red air puppet
dances on

Credits

Some poems in this collection have previously
appeared in college student publications.
Edits and title changes may have taken place since that time.
Needs page 50
Soliloquy 1987, Rocky Mountain College
Billings, Montana
Remnants page 22, *Connected* page 40, *He Knows* page 42
Figments of Imagination 2008 & 2009, Bismarck State College
Bismarck, North Dakota

Come to You Anew page 95, first appeared in
Even Whispered Words Echo:
Lullabies for Dying Children & Other Poems
A project funded in part by a Career Development Grant from the
Lake Region Arts Council and the McKnight Foundation.

Catch-Up page 16 makes reference to
A Prairie Home Companion's Ketchup song.

Layout Design: Clark Gion, Image Printing

Note on the type: Printed in
Anke Calligraphic FG by FontGrube AH
Kiwi School Handwriting by Rob Ashcroft

All images: Dawn Noelle Archer, except pages 20 & 48
Models: Matthew Archer, circa 2001
Dawn (Konietzko) Archer, circa 1987
David Archer, circa 2013
Bob & Vera Archer, circa 1941
Emily & Benjamin Archer, circa 1997

Dawn Noelle Archer has worked with children and families for most of her life. Her time as a Daycare Mom, Pre-school Teacher, Parent Consultant for Windmill Project, and Associate Pastor for United Church of Christ has prepared her well for the journey that is writing.

Dawn is a native of Minnesota, currently resides in North Dakota, but her heart has long belonged to Montana where she met her husband David. They have two adult children, Emily and Matthew.

Remnants of Soul is her second book.

Dawn also authored the children's book *Oh Joy, Bok Choy & Other Greens for Me!*

www.ingramcontent.com/pod-product-compliance
Lightning Source LLC
Chambersburg PA
CBHW060200050426
42446CB00013B/2926